CLIL Readers

Audio available

Our solar system

written by
Mario Castro

Richmond

Since the beginning of time, people have been fascinated by the Sun, the Moon, the stars and other objects in the sky. Ancient astronomers who gazed at the sky noticed that some of the objects moved. They called these objects 'planets'.

Planets orbit the Sun. The planets, their moons and smaller objects such as comets and asteroids also orbit the Sun. They form the solar system.

There are eight planets in the solar system: Mercury, Venus, Earth, Mars, Jupiter, Saturn, Uranus and Neptune.

Our home, Earth, is one of the four rocky planets. The other three are Mercury, Venus, and Mars. The remaining four planets are called 'gas giants' because they lack a solid surface and most of their masses are in the form of gas. They are Jupiter, Saturn, Uranus and Neptune.

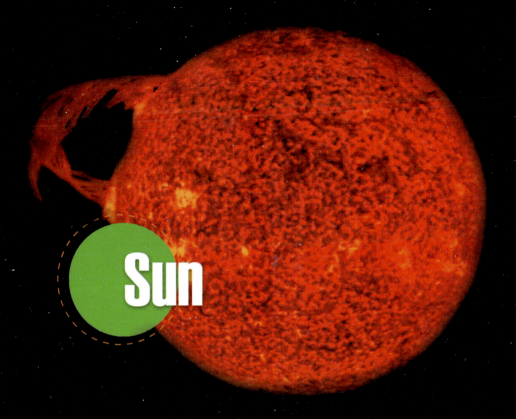

Sun

The Sun is our closest star and it is the centre of the solar system. The Sun has inspired many stories around the world. Some ancient cultures believed the Sun was a god and built temples to worship it.

The Sun supports life on Earth by providing sunlight, which is our primary source of energy. Sunlight allows plants to live and grow. Plants are the main source of food for many animals and people.

The Sun also plays an active role in determining the seasons, ocean currents and the weather.

Mercury

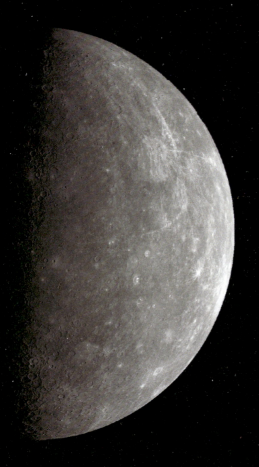

At a distance of almost 58 million kilometres away from the Sun, Mercury is the closest planet to the Sun. The ancient Romans named this small, rocky planet after Mercury, their swift messenger god. This was probably because it moved faster than the other planets, as it travelled around the Sun.

Because it is so close to the Sun, it is extremely hot on Mercury and the planet cannot sustain life. Mercury's surface is full of craters and its atmosphere is thin.

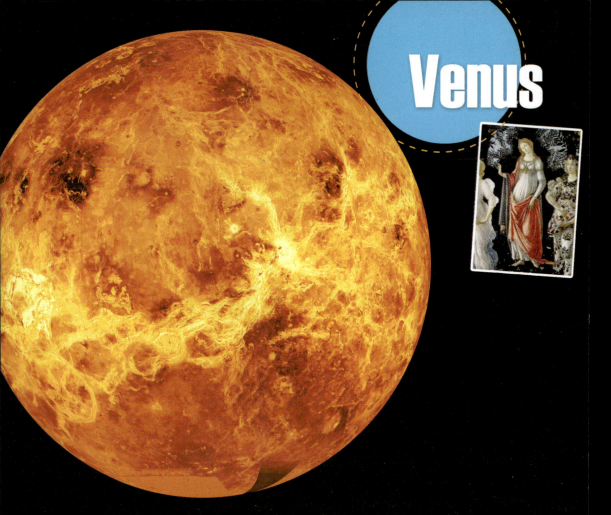

Venus

Venus is the second closest planet to the Sun, at a distance of more than 108 million kilometres. Venus is similar in size and composition to the Earth and it is sometimes referred to as the Earth's twin.

Venus is also close to the Earth and it is covered by clouds that reflect sunlight. For that reason, it appears as the brightest planet in the sky. Because of its beauty, the ancient Romans named this planet after Venus, their goddess of love.

Earth

In third position in distance from the Sun is our home planet, Earth. Its distance from the Sun is almost 150 million kilometres. Earth is the only known planet to have life. Its atmosphere contains air, which together with water provides living things with their basic needs to survive.

Most of our planet is covered by water. When the Sun heats the water in the oceans it becomes water vapour and it goes up into the atmosphere. This causes weather patterns across the planet and the weather conditions we know as rain, snow, storms and others develop.

Mars

Mars is also called the 'red planet'. Its red colour is probably the result of volcanic activity and many dust storms. Mars is the fourth planet from the Sun and the last of the rocky planets. It is about 228 million kilometres away from the Sun.

The ancient Romans associated the colour red with blood, which was one of the symbols of Mars, their god of war. They decided to name the red planet after their god of war.

Jupiter

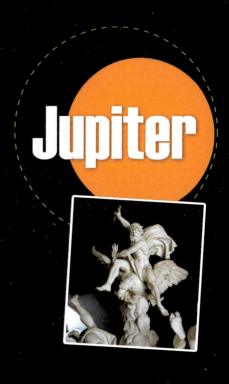

The fifth planet, Jupiter, is the largest planet in the solar system and it is the first of the gas giants. By contrast, most of its forty-nine moons are rocky. Jupiter is more than 778 million kilometres away from the Sun.

The gases that make up Jupiter are mainly hydrogen and helium, which are mainly the same gases that the Sun is made of.

For the ancient Romans, Jupiter was the father of all gods. Because of its size, they named this planet after him.

Saturn

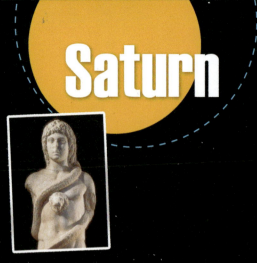

When the ancient astronomers first identified five planets, Saturn was the most distant. Saturn is almost 1,425 million kilometres away from the Sun. It is not as big as Jupiter, but it is also a gas giant made up mostly of hydrogen and helium.

Saturn was the Roman god of agriculture and he was also represented as 'Father Time'. The Romans named the planet after this god because Saturn, the planet, takes a very long time to travel around the Sun.

Uranus

The first planet to be discovered with the help of a telescope was Uranus, which is more than 2,870 million kilometres away from the Sun. It is the seventh planet and like the other gas giants, it is mainly composed of hydrogen and helium and has many moons.

Uranus is also called an 'ice giant' because it contains frozen water in its atmosphere.

Following the Roman tradition, the astronomers who discovered this planet named it after Uranus, the Roman god of the sky and Saturn's father.

Neptune

The last gas giant is also an ice giant because it has water in its atmosphere. There are huge windstorms on Neptune. Some of the storms are the size of Earth! Neptune is about 4,500 million kilometres away from the Sun. It is the eighth and furthest planet from the Sun. It is so far away that it takes Neptune 165 Earth years to complete an orbit of the Sun!

Because of its ocean-blue colour, this planet was named after Neptune, the Roman god of the sea.

Smaller Bodies in the Solar System

Dwarf planets, comets and asteroids are smaller bodies in the solar system.

Dwarf planets are like planets, but much smaller. Although Pluto was first considered to be a planet, in 2006 it was re-named as a dwarf planet. Other dwarf planets are Eris and Ceres.

Asteroids are mostly rocky objects found between Mars and Jupiter. All these objects form a type of belt as they orbit the Sun. They are also known as the 'asteroid belt'.

Comets are very bright when they come close to the Sun and most show a big tail. Probably the most famous comet is Halley's Comet. It usually comes closest to Earth every seventy-six years.

Meteoroids are rocky objects floating in space. When these rocky objects enter the Earth's atmosphere they transform into meteors. The meteors fall towards the ground at high speed quickly disintegrating. We also call falling meteors 'shooting stars' because they look like falling stars in the night sky.

Space Exploration

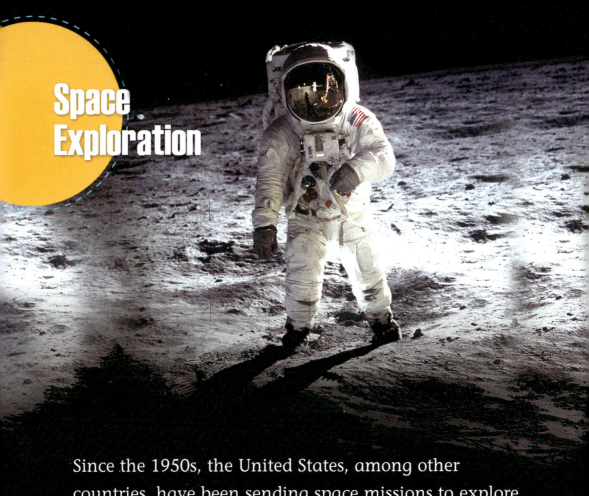

Since the 1950s, the United States, among other countries, have been sending space missions to explore the solar system. The United States was able to send two astronauts to the Moon for the first time in 1969. The two astronauts, Neil Armstrong and Edwin Aldrin, were part of the Apollo 11 mission.

There have been other unmanned missions to most of the planets and their moons. A lot of what we now know about most of the planets and the solar system comes from the photographs that these spacecrafts have sent us during their trips.

Robots have also helped us discover the composition and nature of other planets. For example, Curiosity is a robot that has lived on Mars since 2011. Its mission is to explore the red planet by taking photos. These photos help scientists investigate the possible living conditions on Mars. In the not-too-distant future, perhaps astronauts will be able to land on Mars too.

In the future, space exploration will continue to fascinate people as there are still many hidden mysteries to discover!